ISBN-13: 9798398115987
ISBN-10: 1477123456

Cover design by: Art Painter
Library of Congress Control Number: 2018675309
Printed in the United States of America

CONTENTS

PROLOGUE

As a child, I was fascinated by the magic of transactions. The excitement that came from the neighborhood kids exchanging baseball cards, or the grand spectacle of the weekend garage sales, always intrigued me. Even the simplest act of buying candy from the corner store was a captivating process. The exchange of value for goods was an exhilarating experience that filled me with wonder. This early fascination with sales dynamics turned into a lifelong career, an odyssey across different commerce landscapes that eventually led me to the burgeoning world of legal cannabis.

From being a young entrepreneur knocking on doors to raise money for charities from the neighbors to eventually running a successful boutique agency, The Direct Marketing Concierge, I honed my craft in data-driven direct mail and fully automated sales and marketing programs. Yet, it was the green gold rush, the nascent but rapidly expanding cannabis industry, that beckoned me. Equipped with decades of experience, I stepped into this brave new world, resolved to revolutionize its sales dynamics.

I still remember that day when I stepped into a well-known concentrate company for the first time as their new sales leader. Their sales team was stagnant, disjointed, and uninspired, trying to hit their quotas with no more than a piece of paper with the names of stores they needed to contact each day. I saw an opportunity. I saw a field ripe for harvest but one that was being neglected. It was as if someone had given them seeds and told them there's fertile land out there but left them to figure out how to cultivate the crops.

With my accumulated knowledge and hands-on experience in sales and marketing, I knew it was time to sow the seeds of change. In this book, "The Cannabis Sales Machine," you will learn how I facilitated a transformation, nurturing a disjointed sales team and facilitating a phenomenal growth spurt.

One of the first things I did was implement a CRM system to modernize our sales process. This was followed by reviewing and adjusting the reps' compensation plans to drive the desired behavior. With the creation of actionable reports and weekly meetings, I started shaping a sales force that was no longer disjointed but motivated, efficient, and driven.

Change wasn't easy. It took some effort to convince the team that the new way of doing things would yield better results. Within six months, the positive changes were evident. Sales were growing by a minimum of 10% month over month, the team was working well together, and a spark was lit.

Once the sales engine was purring, I knew it was time to rev up the marketing machine. I started creating booklets for both consumers and buyers about the product offerings. I formalized the on-site training program for retail staff, developed a detailed strategy for in-store support, and developed a robust educational curriculum around all things cannabis, emphasizing Live Resin, the company's primary focus, and more.

The sales and marketing strategies coalesced like well-oiled gears in a machine, their combined force creating a powerful brand presence at all industry events. I then turned my attention to the digital front, creating a social media strategy that doubled their followers in just six months. As the final stroke, I assisted in updating the consumer-facing displays, packaging, and branding.

By the end of my tenure at this concentrate company, the

company was generating a staggering $1,000,000 a month in revenue with the tools and strategies I developed and implemented. 233% growth, from a place where the sales were as stagnant as water in an abandoned well to a dynamic, flowing river of success.

"The Cannabis Sales Machine," therefore, is more than just a book; it's an in-depth guide filled with valuable tools and actionable strategies gleaned from my experiences. Each page is steeped in the wisdom and practical insights that drove a transformation from a stagnant sales environment to a thriving one, from a disjointed team to a harmonized sales force, and from the doldrums to a staggering 233% growth in revenue.

Through the following chapters, you'll be privy to the nuts and bolts of the strategies I deployed. From understanding the fundamentals of CRM implementation to the fine art of aligning sales and marketing, it's all laid bare in this book. You will learn how to transform your sales and marketing tactics to drive incredible growth, create a cohesive team, and build a brand that stands out in the cannabis industry.

Like those youthful transactions that filled me with wonder, this book is an exchange of value. It's a guide that offers the keys to unlocking your potential in the cannabis industry. As you turn each page, I hope you find inspiration to apply these strategies and techniques to your own journey. Let's embark on this voyage together, exploring the grand spectacle of sales and marketing and finding that same sense of wonder that started my journey all those years ago. Now, it's time to open the door to your cannabis sales machine.

CHAPTER 1: WELCOME TO THE WORLD OF WHOLESALE CANNABIS SALES

Welcome to a world where passion and opportunity unite in the fast-growing industry of wholesale cannabis sales. In this book, we will embark on a journey through the heart of the industry, led by an industry veteran with 30 years of successful experience in cannabis sales. With a career filled with milestones, our author has been instrumental in leading several sales teams to triple-digit growth, launching numerous products, and successfully navigating the industry's toughest challenges.

As one of the pioneers of the adult-use cannabis market, our author has spent the last decade at the forefront of the industry's transformation. He has witnessed and played an active role in the dramatic shift from underground culture to a legitimate, mainstream industry. His insights, anecdotes, and expertise provide invaluable knowledge and practical advice for anyone seeking to enter or expand their presence in this exciting and rapidly evolving industry.

Through a captivating narrative that evokes emotions and compels action, this book explores the dynamic world of wholesale cannabis sales, from the early days of underground culture to the present-day complete with state-of-the-art cultivation and distribution networks. The author's vast experience and warm, inviting tone to create a safe and inspiring space to explore and learn from his journey.

Whether you are a budding entrepreneur looking to start a business, a seasoned professional seeking new strategies, or simply curious about the industry, this book has something for you. Join us on this journey as we explore the world of wholesale cannabis sales and discover the keys to unlocking success in this exciting industry.

Meet the Industry Veteran: 30 Years of Cannabis Sales Experience

The author of this book is a true industry veteran, an OG with over 30 years of experience in cannabis sales. But his journey to success in the cannabis industry began long before the legal market emerged. As a young child, he showed an entrepreneurial spirit, selling his used books door-to-door in his neighborhood, his parents recognized his natural talent for sales and knew he would go far.

Over time, he found himself drawn to the cannabis industry, consuming the plant at a young age and beginning to sell it by the time he was just 15 years old. After graduating college, he founded a telemarketing company that helped businesses sell more products and services. This led him into the world of creative marketing and commercial printing, where he became a print broker and sold a million dollars in his first year as a single operator.

But it was his move to Colorado, a state at the forefront of the legal cannabis industry, that truly allowed him to shine. He became an integral part of the adult-use cannabis market, witnessing and playing an active role in the industry's transformation from underground culture to a legitimate, mainstream industry.

Throughout his career, the author has remained passionate about helping small businesses succeed in their sales and marketing efforts. He founded the creative agency Direct Marketing Concierge, which focused on improving results for small businesses' marketing efforts before ultimately selling the company and dedicating himself to the cannabis industry.

CHAPTER 2: THE EVOLUTION OF THE CANNABIS INDUSTRY

From Underground Culture to Legitimate, Mainstream Industry

C annabis has come a long way from its early days as an underground culture. For decades, the use of cannabis was shrouded in mystery and stigma, relegated to the shadows of society. But over the past few decades, that stigma has slowly begun to erode, and cannabis has emerged as a legitimate and increasingly mainstream industry.

Before the legal industry, the cannabis culture was a vibrant and varied landscape of different strains, smoking techniques, and rituals. The cannabis culture had a strong sense of community and camaraderie, fueled by a shared love and appreciation for the plant. It was a culture that celebrated the plant and the people who used it, often in defiance of laws that criminalized it.

As cannabis moved towards legalization and became more mainstream, the culture and community around it also evolved.

The community became more diverse and inclusive, embracing people from all walks of life and backgrounds. The culture shifted from one of rebellion to one of acceptance and openness.

The cannabis industry has proliferated over the past few years, and it is now a multi-billion-dollar industry. The legal cannabis market has emerged in various forms worldwide, from medical marijuana to adult-use cannabis. In many countries, cannabis is no longer considered a dangerous drug but rather a natural medicine with a range of potential benefits.

With the cannabis industry becoming more mainstream, more consumers openly discuss their cannabis consumption and use. This openness has helped to break down further the stigma surrounding cannabis and has contributed to the plant's normalization.

The impact of this openness cannot be overstated. Consumers who are open about their cannabis use are helping to change the public perception of the plant and are paving the way for further legalization and decriminalization efforts. As more people speak out about their experiences with cannabis, more people are becoming educated about its benefits, and more people are joining the movement to legalize it.

The cannabis industry has come a long way from its early days as an underground culture. The cannabis culture before legalization was a vibrant and varied landscape of different strains, smoking techniques, and rituals. Today, cannabis has emerged as a legitimate and increasingly mainstream industry. The normalization of cannabis consumption and use by consumers is helping to change the public perception of the plant and is paving the way for further legalization and decriminalization efforts.

Witnessing and Participating in the Industry's Transformation

The cannabis industry has transformed tremendously over the past decade from an underground culture to a legitimate, mainstream industry. As someone who was part of the industry before legalization, I have witnessed and participated in this transformation, seeing firsthand how the industry has evolved and how sales strategies have changed.

Before the legalization of cannabis, the culture surrounding it was very different. Cannabis was primarily consumed and distributed illegally, often in secret or underground. The industry was characterized by a lack of regulation, an absence of standardized products, and a high level of risk for those involved. The culture of cannabis was rebellious, countercultural, and often associated with criminal activity.

However, as cannabis became legal in more and more states and countries, the industry began to change. With regulation came legitimacy, and with legitimacy came an opportunity for growth and expansion. The industry has become more professional, with standardized products, stricter regulations, and a focus on quality control and safety.

But while the culture of cannabis has changed, many of the same values and attitudes that defined the underground culture have carried over into the legal industry. Many consumers still view cannabis as a way to challenge authority and subvert mainstream culture. Cannabis has become a symbol of rebellion and resistance, even as it becomes more accepted and mainstream.

As the industry has evolved, sales strategies have also had to adapt. In the industry's early days, growers were backpacking their fresh harvests into dispensaries, word of mouth and referrals was a more significant part of the sales process, and small, local networks formed. But as the industry has grown, sales strategies have become more sophisticated. Today, sales are still conducted chiefly in person, and the alignment of sales strategies and marketing is a transformation starting to take place now.

The transformation of the cannabis industry is still ongoing, and we are beginning to see market consolidation as larger companies acquire smaller ones. Vertical integration, once a common strategy in the industry, is starting to disappear. There is simply no way to be an expert at everything, and specialization is becoming more important. Companies are beginning to focus on their core strengths: cultivation, extraction, distribution, or retail.

It is an exciting time to be part of the cannabis industry, and I am looking forward to seeing how the transformations will continue to evolve the industry. One thing is certain: with a solid sales foundation, it will be easier to succeed. The sales strategies that worked in the past may not work in the future, and companies that fail to adapt will be left behind. The key to success in the cannabis industry is to be nimble, adaptable, and always looking for ways to stay ahead of the curve.

CHAPTER 3: THE STATE OF THE WHOLESALE CANNABIS MARKET

*Overview of the current state
of the cannabis industry*

The cannabis industry has been on a rapid upward trajectory in recent years, with the legalization of recreational marijuana use in several states fueling growth in the market. The rise of the recreational market has created new opportunities for businesses to reach a broader customer base, leading to increased demand for cannabis products. Despite this growth, the cannabis industry has faced several challenges, particularly in the flower market. The volatile nature of the flower market has created uncertainty for growers and suppliers, making it difficult to plan and manage their businesses effectively.

In recent months, the cannabis industry has experienced a significant impact due to the COVID-19 pandemic. The initial Covid industry boom led to over-production and a surplus of cannabis products, causing prices to drop dramatically. However, this was followed by a market correction, which has resulted in increased competition and consolidation within the industry. Despite these challenges, the cannabis industry is poised for continued growth in the future. With ongoing legalization efforts and technological advancements, the industry is well-positioned to become a significant player in the global market. Companies that are able to navigate the complexities of the industry and adapt to changing market conditions are well-positioned for success in the years to come.

Opportunities in Wholesale Cannabis:

The world of wholesale cannabis sales is ripe with opportunity, but it also comes with unique challenges. Let's look at both sides in a little more detail.

Rapidly Growing and Evolving Industry

The cannabis industry is one of the fastest-growing industries in the world. It is evolving at a breakneck pace and is full of opportunities for those willing to take on the challenges of working in such a dynamic industry.

Industry Needs More Experienced Talent from Outside the Industry in All Areas

As the industry continues to grow and evolve, there is a growing need for experienced talent from outside the industry in all areas. This includes sales, marketing, finance, and operations. Bringing in talent from outside the industry can bring fresh ideas and best practices from other industries.

Wholesale Sales is the Best Way to Become a Six-Figure Earner in My Opinion

Wholesale sales is the quickest way to become a six-figure earner in the cannabis industry. It requires a solid understanding of the market and the ability to build relationships with buyers and sellers. My father always told me that if you know how to sell, you will always have a job.

Marketing and Advertising Expansion Like All Other Industries

As the industry matures, marketing and advertising are becoming more critical to the success of businesses in the industry. There are many opportunities to develop creative and effective marketing campaigns that resonate with consumers.

Global Expansion

The cannabis industry is rapidly expanding globally, and there are many opportunities to enter new markets and establish a global presence. This can help businesses to diversify their revenue streams and reduce their dependence on any one market. If you are willing to relocate, the opportunities are abundant.

Federal Legalization in the Next 5-10 Years is my Prediction

Many experts predict that federal legalization in the United States is just a few years away. This will open new business opportunities in the cannabis industry, including access to new markets, potential partnerships with large corporations, and interstate commerce.

Establishing a strong brand before federal legalization can provide businesses with a significant advantage. This can build a loyal customer base and create a competitive advantage that can drive growth and potential sales to larger corporate entities.

Establishing a Brand Before Legalization Will Create the Best Opportunity for National Growth and Potential Sale to a Large Corporate Entity (Alcohol, Tobacco, Vape, Pharmaceutical)

Challenges in Wholesale Cannabis:

Compliance is Costly

Compliance with regulations and licensing requirements can be costly and time-consuming. Businesses in the cannabis industry must be prepared to invest heavily in compliance to operate legally and avoid penalties.

Over-Regulation and High Taxation Make it Difficult to be Profitable

The cannabis industry is subject to over-regulation and high taxation, making it challenging for businesses to be profitable. It is essential for companies to carefully manage their expenses and find creative ways to reduce costs. The margins are razor-thin for manufacturers, and over-regulation hurts everyone except the government.

More Competition Every Day

The cannabis industry is becoming increasingly competitive, with new businesses entering the market daily. This requires companies to be agile and innovative to stay ahead of the competition.

Still Some Stigma About Cannabis

Despite the growing acceptance of cannabis, some stigma is still attached to the industry. This can make attracting new customers and investors challenging and may require businesses to be creative in their marketing and outreach efforts. Education is vital in helping change people's minds about cannabis and its benefits.

Must Run a Lean Business to Survive at This Time in the Industry

The cannabis industry is still in its early stages, and businesses must be prepared to run a lean operation to survive. This requires careful management of expenses, a focus on profitability, and a willingness to adapt to changing market conditions.

The opportunities and challenges in wholesale cannabis sales are significant. While the industry is rapidly evolving, having a solid sales foundation is essential so your brand thrives no matter the market conditions.

CHAPTER 4: HIRE

*Building a Successful
Cannabis Sales Team*

Sales talent is the backbone of any successful sales team. They are responsible for generating revenue and driving growth, and we know that only happens once a sale is made at any company. However, finding the right sales talent is easier said than done. Hiring the wrong person for a sales position can significantly impact the company's bottom line. This chapter will discuss the importance of hiring the right sales talent and the high cost of the wrong hire.

The Cost of Hiring the Wrong Person

Hiring the wrong salesperson can be an expensive mistake. According to research, upwards of 35% of the first year's expected earnings is the financial cost of a bad hire. This includes the cost of training, salary, benefits, and lost productivity. Furthermore, it can take up to six months to realize the hire was a mistake. This means that the cost of a wrong hire can quickly add up. Let's break this down real quick. If a rep has an on-target earning potential of $100,000 in year one, hiring the wrong person will cost you upwards of $35,000. This doesn't account for the time wasted by management hiring the wrong person.

Hire slow and fire fast. Take your time finding the right rep, but if you notice they are working out, let this person go. Be swift because they could interfere with your team's growth and success. I suggest a 90-day trial for both sides to ensure it is a fit. Consider a lower pay rate for the 90-day trial; when it works out, the rep gets a little bump in pay.

Time Wasted at the Management Level

Hiring the wrong salesperson can also significantly drain management's time and resources. Managers have to train and coach the new hire, which takes time away from other essential tasks. If the new hire doesn't work out, the process starts all over again, wasting even more time and resources.

Usually, there are a few people involved in the hiring process. This could be the sales leader, an HR person, and the head of the revenue for the company (CEO, CRO, VP of Sales). With the wrong hire, each person involved in the hiring process has lost the time involved in the hiring process. The cost of the wrong hire gets prohibitive when a company's top management is involved. Time is the one resource we can't get back, and time spent on non-revenue-generating activities gets costly very quickly.

How to Avoid Hiring the Wrong Rep

Use a proven, psychological hiring process such as the DISC assessment. DISC is a standard tool for analyzing potential hires to see if they match the benchmark. DISC assesses four areas: Dominance, Influence, Steadiness, and Conscientiousness. Psychological assessments allow you to gain insight into a candidate's personality, work style, and communication skills. Just like a sales process helps to speed up the sales cycle, a hiring process speeds up the time it takes to get the right rep onboarded and earning.

In my past experiences, I struggled with hiring the right sales reps before creating a structured hiring process based on the DISC assessment. Back then, I used to rely solely on how much I enjoyed the conversation during the interview to make my hiring decisions. However, this approach proved to be a costly mistake, as I would soon discover that I had hired the wrong person more often than not. Not only did I have to let them go, but it also meant starting the entire hiring process all over again. This resulted in a loss of time, money, and sales revenue. But as they say, people come into our lives at the right time, and I was fortunate enough to meet a sales consultant at a trade show who became a great friend and mentor. This gentleman introduced me to DISC and taught me how to create a hiring process that always ensures the right hire. Imagine if you could guarantee never hiring the wrong person again for any position.

What would that mean for you, your time, and your business? Yes, implementing these tools may come at a cost, but the time and resources saved in return are worth every penny

CHAPTER 5: TRAIN & ONBOARD

When it comes to the sales process in the cannabis industry, many people tend to overcomplicate things or not have a sales process in place altogether. However, the truth is that the process can be simple if you know what you're doing. The key is to have a well-defined process, which can help you streamline your efforts and shorten the sales cycle. This chapter will discuss the steps involved in the sales process and how you can make the most of each step to improve your sales performance. This is the process I have developed over the past ten years running sales teams in the cannabis space.

Step 1: Research

Research is the most overlooked piece of the sales process, and many sales leaders omit this step in their approach. The first step in the sales process is to conduct thorough research before making contact with potential buyers. This involves finding out what brands you're competing against, the price points of these brands, and what the buyers are looking for. This research can be done online, and it's essential to build your consultative strategy based on the data you gather.

One of the most significant advantages of research is that it can help you shorten the sales cycle. By understanding your target market and what they're looking for, you can tailor your approach to meet their needs and close deals more quickly. I suggest keeping a database of each store, what they carry, and price points. In 90 days, you'll have actionable data to analyze for buying trends, and you will have deep insight into your competitors.

Step 2: Make Contact

Once you've conducted your research, the next step is to contact the potential buyer. This involves going into the store and trying to meet with the buyer. If you can get an introduction to the buyer, this speeds up the process. It's essential to follow the process provided to make further contact and, if possible, get the buyer's cell phone number, as much business in this industry is done over text.

Step 3: Get Samples Approved

To get your foot in the door, you need to create a nice sample pack with more product than required to make a buying decision. Don't be cheap with your sample pack; make it stand out from the rest. Consider a special package just for your samples, don't just send your samples in a brown box. Showcase what makes you different than your competition with your value-add support offerings, such as pop-ups, education, promotions, and any other strategies you have available.

Step 4: Follow Up

Once the samples are delivered, follow up in 1-2 weeks based on the sample process timeline provided by the buyer. It's essential to get feedback from the buyer and share it with the sales team or production team if necessary.

Step 5: Close the Deal

The final step in the sales process is to close the deal. This involves getting a starting order or determining the timeline to get your products on the shelf. If you don't get an order right out of the gate, you probably missed something in your discovery phase that told you there was no opportunity at this time. This happens frequently; you just need to backtrack in your sales process and start again with the prospect.

In conclusion, having a well-defined sales process will help you streamline your efforts and improve your sales performance. It's important to have a trackable process through a CRM, which can help you identify areas for improvement and make adjustments as necessary. Remember to keep the process simple and tweak it as necessary based on the market, state, team, and goals. By following these steps, you will see an immediate improvement in your sales performance.

Communication is the cornerstone of a successful sales team and sales leader. We are in control of our service 100% of the time, and communication is a huge part of providing exceptional service. Without solid communication channels, you will struggle to lead your team effectively. To succeed as a leader, you must know what is happening with all your reps and team members. This is the only way to make informed decisions that benefit your team and business. Lead by example and utilize all your communication tools with your team.

One of the best ways to keep track of all your customer and prospect interactions is in your CRM tool. Your reps should be taking notes on each customer/prospect interaction. A leader can review the notes on their schedule and efficiently support the representatives. When I'm managing a team, I check my reps' notes each night and leave comments for them to review in the morning. This keeps me up to date on what each rep is working on, and I am able to help with any issue a representative may be dealing with. I'm uncovering potential roadblocks and helping the reps shorten the sales cycle or get ahead of a service issue.

In addition to using a CRM, I suggest creating a text group for quick daily communication. It is easy to ask for support via text and get quick responses. Celebrate every win on the text group; this is called "Ringing the Bell." Celebrating the wins creates strong team morale and fosters a sense of community and support among team members.

It is also essential for leaders to have a direct line to the heads of all departments. Leaders need to support their team with all service issues urgently. Remember having direct lines and good working relationships with each department head is extremely important.

When it comes to interacting with customers, leaders should aim to make their reps the hero in the eyes of the customer. This means empowering reps to make decisions and take ownership of their work. When representatives are successful, it reflects well on the entire team and creates a positive image for the business. We all have the right to fail; your reps should understand this.

A company may use a tool like Slack for general company communication. The sales team is often separated from the rest of the company, and tools like Slack help keep the sales team involved in the day-to-day life of the rest of the company. The sales team needs to foster relationships with the team members across the company. Very similar to relationship building in sales. As they say, "It's not about what you know; it's who you know."

In conclusion, communication is crucial to success in life and business. As a leader, you are responsible for creating effective communication channels for you and your team. This includes using a CRM, creating a text group for quick daily communication, and having direct lines and good working relationships with each department head. By making your reps the hero in the eyes of the customer, you will create strong team morale and a successful business.

In today's digital age, businesses rely more on technology to streamline operations and increase efficiency. A **tech stack** is the combination of software and tools companies use to manage their day-to-day operations. The tech stack can include everything from customer relationship management (CRM) software to project management tools and communication software. The right tech stack can help a sales team run more efficiently, reduce costs, and ultimately increase revenue.

Sales teams are the lifeblood of most cannabis businesses, responsible for generating revenue and driving growth. However, without the right tools and technology in place, even the most talented sales teams can struggle to meet their goals. That's where the tech stack comes in.

This includes using a CRM like Pipedrive to manage customer relationships and the sales process, data analysis tools like Excel or Google Sheets to analyze sales data, project management tools like Wrike to keep projects moving forward, communication tools like Slack and text messages to stay in touch with your team and prospects, and marketing automation tools like Ontraport to streamline the marketing and sales process.

By designing a tech stack to meet the needs of your sales team, you will set your team up for success and have the business intelligence at your fingertips to lead your team effectively. With the right tools, sales teams can identify trends, track progress, and adjust their strategy as needed to achieve their goals.

One of the most critical components of a tech stack for sales teams is a Customer Relationship Management tool (CRM). A CRM is a software tool that helps businesses manage customer relationships by providing a centralized database of customer information, including contact information, purchase history, and communication history. You probably have used a CRM throughout your sales career, but if not, I really like Pipedrive.

Pipedrive is an excellent example of a CRM specifically designed for sales teams. It provides sales reps with a visual sales pipeline that helps them manage their sales process and track the progress of each deal. Pipedrive also integrates with other sales tools like email, phone, and social media to provide a complete picture of each customer's interactions with the sales team. Pipedrive is very user-friendly and intuitive, but there are many options out there, and you should research any CRM you think makes sense for your team.

By using a CRM, sales teams can work more efficiently and effectively. They can quickly identify new leads, track their progress through the sales funnel, and prioritize their time and resources accordingly. Your CRM will have a customizable reporting function. Build your reporting to match your sales strategy and the metrics you focus on to drive sales. Refer to the chapter about reporting for the metrics for more information.

Daily activities are required to meet sales targets. Sales is still a numbers game to some degree. As salespeople, we only have so much energy and time to sell each day. This time should be spent on something other than planning. By using the activity tool in your CRM, your days will be planned, and you will get to spend your time selling. Make activity planning a daily habit and watch your efficiency grow.

CHAPTER 6: MANAGE

The Difference Between
Good and Great

R egular sales meetings are an essential aspect of a successful sales team. In fact, the difference between a good and excellent sales team is often their meeting frequency and quality. As a salesperson & sales leader, knowing that you cannot sell in isolation but must work with a team to achieve success is essential. This chapter will explore the importance of regular sales meetings and how they can make a difference in your team's success.

Meetings are where ideas are shared and plans are made. They are also an opportunity to identify and address challenges that may be hindering progress. Sales meetings are a crucial tool in maintaining focus and keeping sales teams accountable.

Here are 12 reasons why sales meetings are effective and critical to your team's success:

1. **Culture** - Sales meetings bring us together to accomplish much more than we could alone. Sales meetings are part

of the foundation that supports a thriving sales culture.

2. **Assessing** - It is essential to measure what is happening in sales (calls, meetings, networking events, etc.) against the plan and continuously analyze the activity's results.

3. **Communication** - Many businesses are plagued with poor communication. The nature of our job requires us to operate like sole proprietors. Without an empowered sales team, a company suffers from fragmented direction and a lack of motivation to execute. More on communication later in the book.

4. **Direction & Numbers** - Numbers are a direct reflection of results. Numbers are the only accurate, impartial measurement of success. They never lie. They are brutally honest. Numbers give us hope, determination, incentive, and recognition for our accomplishments. They also kick us when we need it. Sales meetings are about numbers, and we need to fall in love with numbers.

5. **Motivation** - We are all motivated by different factors. We all have personal forms of internal motivation. Still, peer pressure and competition are potent forms of external motivation that give us that extra spark to jump-start our efforts. Sales meetings create needed competition and pressure. Create an environment of elevation based on competition and collaboration.

6. **Skill set development and reinforcement** - Selling isn't winning. Winning is winning. We win business from the competition by being better. Sales meetings test and hone our abilities, force us to learn and apply new skills and processes that are good for us and make us better than our competition.

7. **Marketing Alignment** - Supercharge your sales and pack your funnels with quality leads by aligning with marketing. Meetings are the best way to remain aligned.

8. **Sharing** - We share what we find and experience in the market. Topics include actual performance compared

with goals and objectives, success stories, opportunities, competitor actions, and sales strategies that work. In addition, this allows for an update on the organization's general health and any changes that have occurred.

9. **Training** - Your team will be more consistent with their messages if you provide them with training on products and services, specific markets, how to fulfill their needs, sales techniques, competitors, and how to sell against them, as well as new processes and technology.

10. **Celebrating Success** - Recognizing and celebrating successes is a decisive element in motivation and team-building. Salespeople are motivated to produce results so they can share them with their peers. These frequent opportunities for positive reinforcement from the Sales Leader and other team members shouldn't be missed.

11. **Consistency** -One of the most critical factors in successful selling is consistency – consistency of effort, consistency in the message, and consistency in the quality and service provided to the customer. This idea of consistency is reinforced when you hold your sales meeting at the same time, on the same day of the week, every week, and when every sales meeting is made up of the same components.

12. **Engagement** - Finally, each meeting needs a fresh injection of fun to engage your reps. This can often be overlooked by sales leaders, creating an environment that stunts growth. Infusing your meetings with fun techniques, roleplay, and movement helps to keep your team engaged and excited to attend weekly meetings. Nothing can drag on your team like stale, recycled meetings. Don't be afraid to switch things up regularly.

It is also important to note that regular sales meetings need not be boring. They can be engaging, fun, and even inspirational. As a sales leader, you should approach sales meetings with a positive attitude and be open to new ideas. Encourage your team members to share their experiences, offer feedback, and ask questions. A sales meeting should be a safe space where everyone feels comfortable speaking their mind and contributing to the team's success. Sales meetings are like visiting Las Vegas. What happens in Vegas, stays in Vegas. The same is true for your sales meetings. Whatever is said remains with the team and doesn't leave the room. If you uncover a rep sharing private information from a meeting with anyone, it needs to be addressed immediately, and this rep may not be suitable for the team.

Regular sales meetings are critical to the success of any sales team. They provide an opportunity for collaboration, goal-setting, progress monitoring, and recognition. Sales meetings should be engaging, fun, and inspiring. They should serve as a platform for sharing ideas and insights. Remember, the difference between a good and excellent sales team may just be the frequency and quality of your sales meetings.

General Meeting Structure

Meetings, meetings, meetings! You've probably been in so many of them that they all seem the same. But, let's face it, the structure of the meetings is important. Although the format may be similar, the time and focus can differ from meeting to meeting. As you and your sales team get into the habit of holding regular sales meetings, you'll learn to adjust the structure to better fit your needs. And let's be honest, who doesn't love a good tailor-made meeting that suits their specific needs?

The 80/20 Rule of Time: Fixating on the Future, Prepared by the Past

- Timing
  - 10% focused on the past (sales results, wins, losses, etc.)

- 10% on the present (current promos, operations updates, etc.)
- 80% building the future (strategies, campaigns, education, etc.)

Structure:

- Results - We live and die by our numbers, and review of the numbers always comes first
- Decision - What decisions need to be discussed for approval from the sales leader
- Discussion - What do you want to discuss related to your sales efforts, clients, issues, other
- Account Review - Weekly granular review of each account to drive towards goal
- On The Radar - Opportunity to discuss anything upcoming personally or professionally that the team or leader needs to be aware of
- Engage - Don't be boring, have fun, switch it up, and watch the engagement of your meetings grow.

The Meetings that have Driven over 100m in Sales & Counting

Weekly Kick-Off Meeting

Let's kick off the week on a high note with an epic meeting! In just 30 minutes, we're going to celebrate our achievements from last week and remind ourselves of the positive impact our hard work has on our customers.

First up, we'll check out the results from the previous week's sales, highlighting and color-coding key indicators of success and areas for improvement. We know that exceptional service is what sets us apart and wins us lifelong customers, so create a priority plan to tackle any unresolved issues from last week. And, of course, if there's anything else that needs attention, work together as a team to reach your goals.

Team Leaders, make sure you have all the necessary data ready to review during the meeting. Reps, bring up any issues you need support with to kickstart the week on the right foot. Remember, we're in this together, and with a positive attitude and teamwork, we can achieve anything!

Example: performance report

Rep	Goal	Total Sales to Date	This Week's Sales	Previous Week's Sales	WoW % Change	% To Goal
Jon	$100,000.00	$50,000.00	$15,000.00	$17,000.00	-13.33%	50.00%
San dy	$50,000.00	$25,000.00	$10,000.00	$7,000.00	30.00%	50.00%
Bill	$25,000.00	$17,000.00	$10,000.00	$5,000.00	50.00%	32.00%
Tot al	$175,000.00	$92,000.00	$35,000.00	$29,000.00	17.14%	52.57%

Weekly 1:1 Coaching Meeting

It's time for your weekly coaching and mentoring session - your chance to boost your reps' skills and knowledge to the next level. I recommend scheduling this meeting at the same time every week.

In this one-hour session, start by reviewing the top-line results of the reps' activities and performance, focusing on the ever-important revenue. Make sure to take notes for each account you review so that we can quantify progress toward the next goal. Your reps should already have data from previous meetings and daily sales reporting, so dive into any accounts that need attention. After the representative shares their insights, review each account on their list, create the next steps for each one, or follow up on previous plans to ensure the reps are on track.

You have all the data needed to review during the meeting, but it's up to the reps to bring their Account Review, Discussion, and On The Radar topics to the table. This is your time to strengthen your relationships with your team members, elevate their skills, motivate them, and make them feel great about themselves.

Weekly Sales Meeting

It's time for the weekly deep dive, where you take 60-90 minutes to motivate and build up the team for even more success.

You'll start by reviewing your numbers as a team, celebrating your wins, and learning from your misses. As the leader, you'll focus on driving the team forward, dissecting your successes to find those little nuggets each rep can use to close more deals. And when things don't go as planned, you'll discuss why and learn from each other's mistakes.

Next up, each rep will list the top 10 deals they're working on for the next week and their value under the Discussion Header. This way, you can track progress and support each other when deals are stalled. Team support is essential for your culture, and it's helpful in difficult situations.

If collections are part of your responsibility, you'll run through it together during this meeting, making plans for the most egregious accounts and keeping collections on track. We work hard as reps, and we want to get our well-earned commissions on time!

Let's not forget about marketing initiatives! We'll train on anything new that's been developed and brainstorm ideas for what we'd like to see developed. When sales and marketing are aligned, your goals will be exceeded. Consider taking 15min at each meeting for the marketing team to come in and discuss what's in the works and help with the alignment. More on Alignment later in the book.

Lastly, you're going to mix things up and bring something new and fun to the meeting each week. You could train on overcoming objections or do a fun activity to improve teamwork. As the leader, you promise to keep things fresh and allow your meetings to evolve over time, creating an environment of growth in the minds of your reps.

Remember, you'll have all the data you need to review during the meeting, but it's up to the reps to bring their Decisions, Discussion, and On The Radar topics to the table.

Reporting & Business Intelligence

As a sales leader, your ultimate goal is to drive growth and revenue for your organization. To achieve this, you need to have a clear understanding of where your sales team stands and where it needs to go. This is where data analysis comes in. By leveraging business intelligence, you can gain insights into your sales performance and make informed decisions to drive growth. This chapter will explore the key data points every sales leader should focus on to manage their team and achieve their goals effectively. I will share an example of a Daily Sales Report you can recreate.

The Importance of Data Analysis:

Sales is a data-driven function, and data analysis is critical to sales success. Sales leaders cannot make informed decisions or identify trends and patterns that could impact their team's performance without accurate and relevant data. Moreover, with the increasing amount of data available today, it's more important than ever to filter and analyze data to extract insights that can drive growth. By leveraging business intelligence, sales leaders can gain a competitive advantage and stay ahead of the curve.

Key Data Points for Sales Management:

When managing a sales team, there are several key data points that every sales leader should be aware of. These data points can help you track your team's progress, identify areas of improvement, and make informed decisions. Here are some of the critical data points that I look at when managing a sales team:

Daily sales numbers by rep and team:

Tracking daily sales numbers can help you identify trends and patterns in your team's performance. Tracking sales by rep and team, you can see who is performing well and who needs additional coaching and support.

Month-to-date sales:

Tracking month-to-date sales can help you measure your team's progress toward your revenue goals. It's important to include a percentage-to-goal metric to help you see how close you are to achieving your targets.

SKU Data:

Tracking the number of units sold can help you understand your team's sales volume and identify growth opportunities. Tracking every SKU you offer to get a complete picture of your team's performance is essential. Tracking SKU data can help you identify which products are selling well and which are not. It's important to track total units sold for the year and month-to-date, as well as a year-over-year comparison to identify trends and patterns. You can get very granular with each customer and how the SKUs are performing at a given store. Then you can create a growth plan for each customer.

Collections:

Tracking collections can help you manage your cash flow and ensure you are paid on time. It's important to track both month-to-date and year-to-date collections, as well as what's due this week and what's overdue.

Customer data:

Tracking customer data can help you understand your customers' buying behavior and preferences. It's essential to track which SKUs they purchase, their month-to-date purchases, and year-over-year purchase history to identify opportunities for cross-selling, upselling, and trends by SKU.

Example of Daily Sales Report:

Data analysis is critical to sales success, and sales leaders must leverage business intelligence to gain insights into their team's performance and make informed decisions. Sales leaders can effectively manage their teams and drive growth by tracking key data points such as daily sales numbers, month-to-date sales, number of units sold, collections, SKU data, and customer data. Remember, if you don't know where you are, you can't get to where you want to be. So, start tracking your data today and gain the insights you need to achieve your goals.

	Rep 1	Rep 2	Rep 3	Grand Totals
Previous Days Sales Revenue				$0.00
Daily Sales Revenue				$0.00
MTD Sales Revenue	$12,292.85	$66,074.34	$17,805.00	$96,172.19
Rep Goal	$100,000.00	$50,000.00	$50,000.00	$200,000.00
Rep % to Goal	12%	132%	36%	48%
Cartridges	244	856	280	1,380
Concentrates	311	3,110	1,010	4,431
Out The Door	$11,970.35	$61,754.01	$16,192.50	$89,916.86
Awaiting Delivery		$4,370.24	$1,637.50	$6,007.74
Sample Orders	2	24		26
Current orders in LL		46	7	53
Collections				
MTD	$54,772.73	$39,303.21	$15,725.00	$109,800.94
YTD	$536,635.07	$172,054.68	$80,632.97	$789,322.72
Largest Daily Order/Rep:		Rep 1: $5,700		

You are flying blind if you aren't developing reporting from the sales data you can access. Turn your data into actionable business intelligence for the team. You probably have enough data to build a predictive report of when customers must reorder to keep the shelves stocked. As a sales leader, you must become a proficient data analyst.

CHAPTER 7: MOTIVATE

Strategies for Empowering
Sales Teams

M otivating and empowering your sales team is crucial for the success of your business. Here are some effective strategies that can help you achieve this goal:

1. Offer Fair and Adequate Compensation: Compensation is a critical factor that drives sales reps' behavior. Sales reps should be given the opportunity to earn a higher income based on their performance. They should be the highest-paid employees in the company. Ensure that they are compensated fairly and adequately for their work. They can be motivated by rewards beyond cash, such as time off, public recognition, and opportunities to share or lead.

2. Make Them Feel Valued: Involve your sales team in the decision-making process. Seek their opinions and ideas. This makes them feel valued and empowers them to take ownership of their work. Offer growth and advancement opportunities to help them progress in their careers.

3. Celebrate Small Wins: Celebrate small achievements

publicly. Recognize a meeting that was landed or move a prospect to the next stage in the sales process. It is a great way to boost their mood and keep them motivated.

4. Educate Your Team: Encourage your sales reps to learn more about the business, industry, and products they sell. Build education into your monthly management strategy, and provide books and educational content to the team.

5. Be Flexible: Every sales rep has different needs and preferences for communication. Modify your management strategy by the representative, and be flexible in your approach.

By implementing these strategies and others you like, you will motivate and empower your sales team to achieve great results for your business.

Compensation Drive Behavior

Sales compensation plans are critical to the success of any organization, as they motivate sales representatives to perform better and meet their targets. An effective sales compensation plan ensures that sales representatives are fairly compensated for their efforts and incentivizes them to work harder to increase their earnings. This chapter will discuss the various types of sales compensation plans and how they impact sales performance.

Types of Sales Compensation Plans

1. Straight Salary

A straight salary plan involves paying a fixed salary to sales representatives, irrespective of their performance. This plan is typical in industries with long sales cycles or little control over the sales process. Straight salary plans are usually used for entry-level positions or sales representatives responsible for maintaining existing accounts rather than acquiring new business. This is not the right strategy to drive growth.

2. Salary + Commission

Salary plus commission plans are the most common type of sales compensation plan. Sales representatives receive a fixed salary plus a commission on the revenue they generate. This plan provides sales representatives with a guaranteed income while incentivizing them to perform better and increase their earnings. If any of your reps are not motivated by money, they aren't suitable for your team or sales in general. The commission percentage may vary depending on the industry, product, or service being sold and the level of difficulty in making the sale.

3. Salary + Commission + Bonus

A salary plus commission plus bonus plan is a great way to attract talent and provide strong incentives for the team to strive for. I suggest a combination of individual and team bonus opportunities. The bonus is usually awarded based on achieving specific performance targets, such as exceeding sales targets or acquiring new customers. This plan motivates sales representatives to exceed their targets and rewards them accordingly.

Best Practices for Sales Compensation Plans

1. Keep it Simple and Concise

Sales compensation plans should be simple and easy to understand. Complicated plans can confuse and demotivate sales representatives, leading to reduced performance. The plan should clearly outline the sales targets, the commission rates, and the bonus structure. The more complex the program, the more time the sales leader spends managing payroll.

2. Pay on Time

Sales representatives work hard to achieve their targets and expect to be compensated on time. Late payments can demotivate sales representatives and affect their performance.

Organizations should ensure that payments are made on time and communicate any delays clearly. I had an owner tell me he wasn't going to pay me what we agreed upon because it was too much money. This wasn't fair to me, and I left the company. Just don't mess with your team's pay outside of your review periods.

3. Use Data to Drive Decision Making

Sales compensation plans should be based on data and analytics. Organizations should use data to determine the sales targets and bonus structure. This ensures that the program is aligned with the organization's goals and objectives and motivates sales representatives to perform better. Commission rates should be in line with the industry and your competition.

Sales compensation plans are critical to the success of any organization. The type of plan chosen depends on the industry, product, or service being sold and the level of difficulty in making the sale. Organizations should keep the plan simple and concise, pay on time, and use data to drive decision-making. Sales representatives should be well compensated for their efforts, and the compensation plan should incentivize them to perform better and increase their earnings. Remember, like anything else in life, you get what you pay for.

CHAPTER 8: THE SECRET SAUCE

Sales and Marketing Alignment

In the competitive landscape of the cannabis industry, effective sales and marketing strategies are essential for business success. This is the Secret Sauce that many companies are not focused on or taking advantage of. Sales and marketing alignment is crucial to ensuring that both teams work together to achieve common goals. It takes so little to be better than the competition, and the alignment of sales and marketing is a great way to stand out. This chapter will discuss the importance of sales and marketing alignment and how businesses can achieve it.

The Importance of Sales and Marketing Alignment

From experience, I can tell you that sales and marketing alignment can add 35% annual growth to your business. Why so many companies don't prioritize this alignment will always make me scratch my head. In the cannabis industry, where regulatory restrictions can limit traditional marketing methods, sales and marketing alignment is necessary to stand out in creative and unique ways. Creating shared goals and bonus opportunities will drive the collaboration between the teams needed to develop effective alignment.

One way to achieve sales and marketing alignment is to focus on regular educational content. Cannabis is a complex product; there are many different products made in various ways that need to be explained. From THC to terpenes, to how different strains can affect you, and much more. Education is a great and effective way to strengthen your brand following. Sales and marketing teams can collaborate to create educational content that addresses consumer and buyer questions and concerns. This content can be in the form of blogs, videos, social media posts, and other digital media. Ask your buyers what content they would benefit from and provide it to them. This is a great way to add value and do something many companies need to do.

Another aspect of sales and marketing alignment is the promotion of each product offered. Sales teams should work closely with marketing teams to create product-specific flyers or a one sheet. Consider a little booklet of all your product offerings, like a mini catalog. These pieces of collateral highlight each product's benefits and unique selling points. Every time a new piece of collateral is developed, it creates an opportunity to go back in and speak with your buyers. Marketing teams can create eye-catching packaging and point-of-purchase materials that draw attention to each product. A sales rep's insight about how to stand out in the retail environment is invaluable to the marketing team.

Visual merchandising is an underutilized tool in the cannabis industry. However, statistics show that images significantly influence consumer purchasing decisions. Did you know that 67% of consumers say images are super important in purchasing decisions, and 65% of individuals say they are visual learners? Furthermore, 63% of consumers say product descriptions are less important than images. These statistics highlight the importance of visual merchandising in the cannabis industry. Visual merchandising can help businesses create an immersive experience that engages customers and drives sales.

Good visual merchandising can increase message retention by up to 42%. This means that customers are more likely to remember your brand and products if they are presented in an engaging and visually appealing way. Visual merchandising provides businesses with a way to communicate with customers without relying on traditional marketing methods.

Types of Visual Merchandising Tools

Visual merchandising tools can include displays, product showcases, window clings, door wraps, wall wraps, fridge wraps, floor stickers, 3D signage, banners, and more. These tools should be used to enhance the customer experience and create an immersive environment that showcases your products.

Developing a Visual Merchandising Strategy

If you don't have a visual merchandising strategy in place, it is highly recommended that you develop one. Your strategy should include all the ways you can merchandise a store and how your program works. Create a piece of collateral that showcases your visual merchandising program to assist in gaining approval to merchandise. I suggest creating a piece of collateral that 'WOWs' everyone you show it to.

Your visual merchandising should be educational and eye-catching, making your brand stand out among all the other noise in every store. It should also align with your branding and marketing messaging to create a consistent customer experience. Your sales team should promote your visual merchandising program to retailers to ensure it is implemented effectively.

Consider a bonus for getting stores online with your visual merchandising program.

By developing a solid visual merchandising strategy, businesses can create a compelling argument for retailers to allocate space for their products. Some stores have already started to generate revenue streams from selling space in their stores to brands. You will have to decide if the fees a store may charge are worth it based mainly on the account size. If the account is small but has a lot of foot traffic, consider paying their fees. As a sales leader, you should have the business intelligence readily available to analyze the opportunity financially.

Sales campaigns are another way sales and marketing teams can work together to drive revenue. Creating targeted sales campaigns that align with marketing messaging gives your team a reason to go in and talk with a buyer that isn't the same old tired pitch. Your campaigns should run for a set time (60-90 days), and they must be quantifiable so you can audit each campaign to improve on the next campaign. These campaigns can include promotions, discounts, limited-time offers that incentivize customers to make a purchase, and any other ideas your team can develop that make you stand out from the competition.

Branding is an essential aspect of sales and marketing alignment. Sales and marketing teams must work together to create a consistent brand message that resonates with customers. Branding should be building a loyal following, and as I discussed earlier, education is one of the most effective ways to aid in branding.

Social media and advertising are other critical areas of sales and marketing alignment. Social media platforms like Instagram and Twitter are effective marketing channels allowing businesses to connect with customers and build brand awareness. Twitter now allows the advertising of THC-based products. Time will tell if

Twitter will become the leading national advertising platform for cannabis. Sales and marketing teams can work together to create targeted advertising campaigns that align with marketing messaging and sales goals.

Quantifiable alignment is essential to track the effectiveness of sales and marketing strategies. Metrics, such as website traffic, social media engagement, and sales revenue, can be used to measure the success of sales and marketing campaigns. Sales and marketing teams should regularly review these metrics to identify areas of improvement and adjust their strategies accordingly.

Sales and marketing alignment is crucial to sales success in the competitive cannabis industry. Businesses can create compelling sales and marketing strategies by focusing on educational content, product promotion, point-of-purchase materials, visual merchandising tools, sales campaigns, branding, social media, and advertising. Quantifiable alignment is essential to track the effectiveness of your strategies. The cannabis industry is a rapidly evolving landscape, and businesses that achieve sales and marketing alignment are better equipped to navigate the challenges and succeed.

ABOUT THE AUTHOR

Lee Weiner

Imagine sailing smoothly through the rough waters of the competitive cannabis industry, confidently hitting your revenue goals while your sales and marketing strategy works like a well-oiled machine. Sounds appealing, right? The good news is— it's entirely achievable. And I'm here to help you get there.

I'm your trusted guide with over three decades in the cannabis industry, weathering its storms and witnessing its trends. With my hands-on experience, I've spurred substantial growth, scaling sales beyond $100 Million and consistently achieving triple-digit growth. Navigating this challenging terrain has not only given me deep insights but also honed my skills in crafting powerful sales and marketing strategies.

However, the journey doesn't stop at cannabis. Before venturing into this vibrant industry, I headed a direct marketing and printing company, empowering small businesses across the nation to elevate their marketing efforts. Merging data-driven direct mail campaigns, personalized digital engagement, and comprehensive automated marketing programs, we ignited the power of sales teams. This diverse experience shapes my holistic approach, offering you the best of both worlds.

The key to unlocking revenue goals lies in seamlessly integrating sales and marketing—a process that might appear complex but can be made simple. That's where I come in. Together, we'll create a compelling narrative that resonates with your customers and fuels sales growth, leaning on my expertise in the cannabis industry and direct marketing.

Don't let roadblocks in sales management become stumbling blocks to your success. Let's collaboratively devise an integrated sales and marketing strategy to catapult your growth and maximize your returns. The future of your cannabis company can be bright—we just have to build it together.

Eager to turn this vision into reality? Reach out today, and let's discuss how my sales consulting services can help your business to not just meet but surpass its revenue goals. The journey towards success starts with a single step

—let's take that step together.

BOOKS BY THIS AUTHOR

Roi Marketing Secrets Revealed

ROI Marketing Secrets Revealed is a collective MasterMind effort of 36 of Americas leading marketing experts to show you the value of determining ROI (return on investment) for your business. By focusing on ROI for each dollar spent in your marketing program, you can calculate how much you are spending on every marketing alternative. You can see in clear numbers which marketing channel is producing the most return for your invested dollars. Once you know this number, you can use it to compare every dollar you spend on marketing to determine which marketing strategy produces the best return for your business. Your newfound ROI knowledge will allow you to intelligently shift your money to your most effective marketing options, slash wasted expenses that don't produce, and increase the number of prospects you get for every dollar you spend.

www.ingramcontent.com/pod-product-compliance
Lightning Source LLC
Chambersburg PA
CBHW070838220526
45466CB00002B/814